Table Of Contents

Chapter 1: Introduction to AI-Generated Video Content Creation   3

    The Rise of Generative AI in Creative Industries   4

    Benefits of Using AI for Video Content Creation   5

    Overview of AI-Generated Video Creation Tools and Platforms   7

Chapter 2: AI-Generated Video Content Creation in Action   11

    AI-Generated Special Effects and Visual Enhancements   12

    AI-Generated Marketing Campaigns and Advertisements   14

    AI-Generated Virtual Reality Experiences   15

Chapter 3: Exploring AI-Generated Music Composition and Production   18

    How AI is Revolutionizing Music Composition   19

    AI-Generated Music Production Tools and Software   22

    Examples of AI-Generated Music in the Industry   24

Chapter 4: AI's Impact on Graphic Design, Digital Art, and Fashion   26

AI-Generated Graphic Design Techniques   27

AI in Fashion Design and Trend Forecasting   28

AI-Generated Digital Art and Illustration   31

Chapter 5: AI-Generated Storytelling, Narrative Creation, and Product Design   33

AI-Generated Storytelling Techniques   34

AI in Product Design and Prototyping   35

Examples of AI-Generated Narratives and Products   37

Chapter 6: The Future of AI in Interior Design, Architecture, and Advertising   40

AI-Generated Interior Design Concepts   41

AI in Architecture and Building Design   43

AI-Generated Advertising Content and Campaigns   44

Chapter 7: AI's Role in Social Media Content Creation and Education   47

AI-Generated Social Media Content Strategies   48

AI in Education and Training Simulations   50

Examples of AI-Generated Educational Content   52

Chapter 8: Conclusion and Looking Ahead   54

Ethical Considerations in AI-Generated Content Creation   55

Future Trends in AI-Generated Video Content and Beyond   57

Final Thoughts on the Ultimate Guide to AI-Generated Video Content Creation   59

01

Chapter 1: Introduction to AI-Generated Video Content Creation

The Rise of Generative AI in Creative Industries

As technology continues to advance at a rapid pace, generative AI is revolutionizing the way creative industries operate. From video content creation to music composition, virtual reality experiences to fashion design, AI is becoming an invaluable tool for artists and creators. Companies are leveraging AI to streamline their workflows, create high-quality content, and stay ahead of the competition in an ever-evolving digital landscape.

One of the most prominent uses of generative AI in creative industries is in video content creation. Major studios are utilizing AI to automate tasks like lip-syncing actors' performances in multiple languages, creating deepfake avatars for marketing campaigns, and generating special effects that would have been time-consuming and costly to produce manually. This technology is not only saving time and resources but also pushing the boundaries of what is possible in the world of visual storytelling.

AI-generated music composition and production is another area where generative AI is making a significant impact. By analyzing vast amounts of data and identifying patterns, AI algorithms can create unique and original music compositions that resonate with audiences. This has opened up new possibilities for musicians and composers looking to experiment with different genres and styles, as well as for brands looking to enhance their marketing campaigns with custom-made soundtracks.

In addition to video and music, generative AI is also being used to create immersive virtual reality experiences that blur the lines between reality and fiction. By harnessing the power of AI, creators can design virtual worlds that respond to user input in real-time, offering a truly interactive and engaging experience for users. This technology has the potential to revolutionize industries like gaming, education, and training by providing a more personalized and dynamic learning environment.

Overall, the rise of generative AI in creative industries is transforming the way artists and creators work, pushing the boundaries of what is possible in terms of content creation and storytelling. With AI-generated video content, music compositions, virtual reality experiences, and more, companies can stay ahead of the curve and deliver high-quality, engaging content to their audiences. As this technology continues to evolve, we can expect to see even more innovative uses of generative AI in the creative world, shaping the future of digital content creation.

Benefits of Using AI for Video Content Creation

The benefits of using AI for video content creation are numerous and varied, making it an invaluable tool for individuals and companies alike. One of the key advantages of leveraging AI in this process is the ability to save time and resources. With AI-powered tools, tasks that would traditionally take hours or even days to complete can now be done in a fraction of the time, allowing content creators to focus on more important aspects of their work.

Additionally, AI can help enhance the quality of video content by providing advanced editing capabilities that would otherwise require extensive training and expertise. From color correction to special effects, AI can automate tedious tasks and ensure a professional finish to videos. This not only improves the overall aesthetic appeal of the content but also helps maintain consistency across different projects.

Another significant benefit of using AI for video content creation is the ability to personalize and customize content for specific audiences. AI algorithms can analyze data and user behavior to tailor videos to individual preferences, increasing engagement and driving conversion rates. This level of personalization can be especially beneficial in marketing campaigns, where targeted messaging can make a significant impact on ROI.

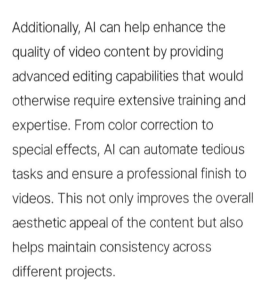

Moreover, AI can assist in generating creative ideas and concepts for video content, providing inspiration and innovation to content creators. By analyzing data trends and consumer behavior, AI can suggest new angles and approaches to storytelling, helping creators stay ahead of the curve and produce content that resonates with their audience.

Overall, the benefits of using AI for video content creation are vast and diverse, making it an indispensable tool for anyone looking to produce high-quality, engaging videos. From saving time and resources to enhancing the quality of content and personalizing it for specific audiences, AI is revolutionizing the way videos are created and consumed in the digital age. For people looking for a comprehensive guide on AI-generated video content creation, understanding these benefits is essential to harnessing the full potential of this groundbreaking technology.

Overview of AI-Generated Video Creation Tools and Platforms

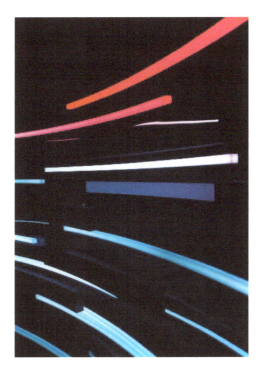

As the demand for high-quality video content continues to grow, companies are turning to AI-generated video creation tools and platforms to streamline their production process. These tools leverage the power of artificial intelligence to automate tasks such as editing, special effects, and even entire marketing campaigns. This allows businesses to create professional-looking videos at a fraction of the time and cost of traditional methods.

Generative AI is revolutionizing the creative industries by enabling companies to generate high-quality video content, special effects, and even entire marketing campaigns. Major studios are increasingly turning to AI for tasks like lip-syncing actors' performances in different languages and creating deepfake avatars for training and marketing purposes. This technology is not only improving efficiency but also opening up new possibilities for creativity and innovation in the industry.

The Ultimate Guide to AI-Generated Video Content Creation

In addition to video creation, AI is also making waves in other creative fields such as music composition, virtual reality experiences, graphic design, storytelling, fashion design, product design, interior design, advertising, social media content creation, education, and training simulations. These AI-generated tools are helping businesses stay ahead of the competition by producing cutting-edge content that resonates with their audience.

One of the key benefits of using AI-generated video creation tools is the ability to scale production quickly and efficiently. These platforms are capable of generating a large volume of content in a short amount of time, allowing businesses to keep up with the ever-increasing demand for video content across various platforms. This scalability is especially important for companies looking to expand their reach and engage with their audience on a global scale.

Overall, AI-generated video creation tools and platforms are revolutionizing the way businesses approach content creation. By leveraging the power of artificial intelligence, companies can create high-quality videos that resonate with their audience and drive engagement. Whether it's for marketing campaigns, training simulations, or social media content, AI is transforming the creative industries and opening up new possibilities for businesses looking to stay ahead of the curve.

02

Chapter 2: AI-Generated Video Content Creation in Action

AI-Generated Special Effects and Visual Enhancements

AI-generated special effects and visual enhancements are revolutionizing the way video content is created and consumed. With the advancements in generative AI technology, companies are now able to generate high-quality video effects that were once only possible through expensive and time-consuming manual methods. From creating realistic explosions to seamless green screen compositing, AI is changing the game for visual effects artists.

One of the most exciting applications of AI-generated special effects is in the film industry. Major studios are now using AI to enhance their films with stunning visual effects that were previously out of reach. For example, AI can be used to create lifelike simulations of natural disasters, futuristic landscapes, and even alien creatures. This technology is allowing filmmakers to bring their wildest visions to life on the big screen with unprecedented realism.

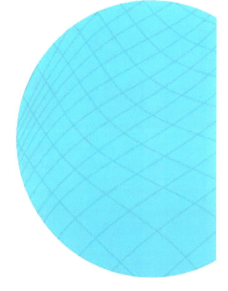

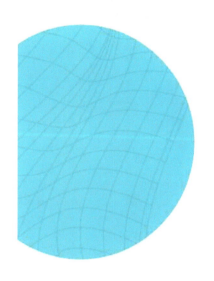

In addition to film, AI-generated special effects are also making waves in the advertising industry. Brands are using AI to create eye-catching visuals that capture the attention of consumers and drive engagement. Whether it's a dynamic product demonstration or a captivating brand story, AI-generated special effects are helping companies stand out in a crowded marketplace.

Another exciting application of AI-generated special effects is in virtual reality experiences. By using AI to enhance VR environments with realistic textures, lighting, and animations, developers can create immersive worlds that feel truly lifelike. This technology is opening up new possibilities for interactive storytelling, training simulations, and educational experiences that were previously limited by technical constraints.

Overall, AI-generated special effects and visual enhancements are pushing the boundaries of creativity and innovation in a wide range of industries. From film and advertising to VR and education, the possibilities are endless with this groundbreaking technology. By harnessing the power of AI, content creators can bring their ideas to life in ways that were once thought impossible, revolutionizing the way we experience video content.

AI-Generated Marketing Campaigns and Advertisements

In today's digital age, AI technology has made significant advancements in various industries, including marketing and advertising. Generative AI is revolutionizing the way companies create content, with the ability to generate high-quality video content, special effects, and entire marketing campaigns. This technology is being embraced by major studios for tasks such as lip-syncing actors' performances in different languages and creating deepfake avatars for training and marketing purposes.

One of the most exciting applications of AI-generated content is in music composition and production. AI algorithms can analyze music trends and patterns to create original compositions that resonate with audiences. This can be a game-changer for musicians and music producers looking to innovate and stay ahead of the curve in a competitive industry.

AI-generated virtual reality experiences are also gaining traction, allowing companies to create immersive and interactive content that engages users in new and exciting ways. From virtual tours of real estate properties to interactive training simulations, the possibilities are endless with AI technology.

In the world of graphic design and digital art, AI is being used to create stunning visuals and illustrations that captivate audiences. From logo design to digital paintings, AI algorithms can generate unique and eye-catching designs that help brands stand out in a crowded marketplace.

When it comes to advertising content and campaigns, AI-generated content can provide marketers with valuable insights and data-driven strategies to optimize their campaigns for maximum impact. By analyzing consumer behavior and preferences, AI can help companies create personalized and targeted ads that resonate with their target audience. This level of customization and precision can lead to higher conversion rates and increased ROI for businesses.

AI-Generated Virtual Reality Experiences

AI-generated virtual reality experiences are revolutionizing the way we interact with digital content. By combining the power of artificial intelligence with immersive technologies like VR headsets, users can now step into completely virtual worlds that are generated in real-time based on their actions and preferences. This opens up a whole new realm of possibilities for entertainment, training, and even therapy.

One of the key advantages of AI-generated virtual reality experiences is the ability to create personalized and adaptive content. Through machine learning algorithms, these systems can analyze user behavior and preferences to dynamically adjust the environment and storyline to provide a more engaging and tailored experience. This level of personalization is not possible with traditional pre-rendered content, making AI-generated VR experiences truly unique and interactive.

Moreover, AI-generated virtual reality experiences are also being used in education and training simulations. By simulating real-life scenarios in a virtual environment, students and professionals can practice and improve their skills in a safe and controlled setting. This is particularly valuable for high-risk professions like surgery or aviation, where mistakes can have serious consequences. With AI-generated VR experiences, learners can gain practical experience without any real-world risks.

In the entertainment industry, AI-generated virtual reality experiences are pushing the boundaries of storytelling and immersion. By creating lifelike characters and environments that react to user inputs in real-time, content creators can deliver truly immersive and interactive narratives that blur the line between reality and fiction. This level of engagement is attracting a new generation of audiences who crave more interactive and personalized content.

Overall, AI-generated virtual reality experiences are a game-changer in the creative industries. From entertainment to education, businesses are leveraging the power of AI to create compelling and engaging virtual experiences that push the boundaries of what is possible. As this technology continues to evolve, we can expect to see even more innovative applications that will redefine how we interact with digital content in the future.

03

Chapter 3: Exploring AI-Generated Music Composition and Production

How AI is Revolutionizing Music Composition

In recent years, artificial intelligence (AI) has made significant advancements in various industries, including the creative sector. Generative AI, in particular, has been making waves in music composition, revolutionizing the way music is created and produced. Companies are now using AI algorithms to generate high-quality music content, from simple melodies to complex symphonies, in a fraction of the time it would take a human composer. This technology is changing the landscape of the music industry, allowing for faster and more efficient production of music across genres.

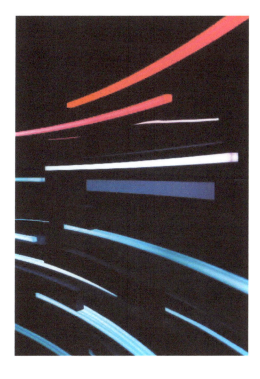

One of the key advantages of AI-generated music composition is its ability to analyze vast amounts of music data and learn from it to create original compositions. These algorithms can mimic the style and characteristics of famous composers or generate entirely new and unique pieces that push the boundaries of traditional music. This opens up new opportunities for artists and producers to experiment with different sounds and styles, leading to a more diverse and innovative musical landscape.

AI-generated music is also being used in film, television, and advertising, where composers can quickly create custom music tracks that perfectly match the tone and style of a project. This has not only streamlined the production process but has also enabled smaller productions with limited budgets to access high-quality music content that would have been otherwise out of reach. The versatility of AI-generated music makes it a valuable tool for content creators looking to enhance their projects with professional and original music compositions.

The Ultimate Guide to AI-Generated Video Content Creation

In addition to music composition, AI is also revolutionizing the way music is produced and mixed. AI algorithms can analyze audio tracks and automatically adjust levels, balance frequencies, and even apply effects to create a polished and professional sound. This reduces the time and effort required to produce high-quality music, allowing artists and producers to focus on the creative aspects of their work rather than technical details. AI-driven production tools are becoming increasingly popular in recording studios, providing musicians with innovative ways to enhance their music production process.

Overall, AI-generated music composition is reshaping the music industry, offering new possibilities for artists, producers, and content creators. By harnessing the power of AI algorithms, musicians can create music faster, experiment with new styles, and access professional production tools that were once reserved for top-tier studios. As the technology continues to evolve, we can expect to see even more groundbreaking advancements in music composition and production, further blurring the lines between human creativity and artificial intelligence.

AI-Generated Music Production Tools and Software

In recent years, AI technology has been revolutionizing the music industry with the development of AI-generated music production tools and software. These innovative tools use machine learning algorithms to analyze and replicate musical patterns, enabling users to create high-quality music compositions with minimal effort. Whether you're a professional musician looking to streamline your workflow or an amateur producer looking to experiment with new sounds, AI-generated music production tools offer a wide range of possibilities for creating unique and innovative music.

One of the key benefits of AI-generated music production tools is their ability to generate music quickly and efficiently. By analyzing vast amounts of musical data, these tools can generate melodies, harmonies, and rhythms that are both original and engaging. This can be particularly useful for musicians who are looking to overcome creative blocks or explore new musical ideas. Additionally, AI-generated music production tools can help musicians collaborate with others by providing a platform for sharing and remixing music in real-time.

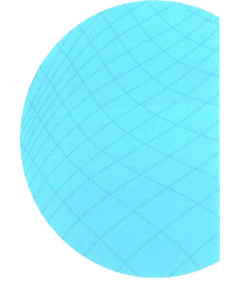

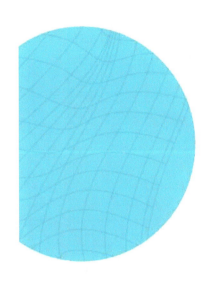

Furthermore, AI-generated music production tools can enhance the overall quality of music compositions by providing advanced editing and mixing capabilities. These tools can automatically adjust tempo, pitch, and dynamics to create a polished and professional sound. Additionally, AI-generated music production tools can help musicians experiment with different genres and styles by providing a wide range of customizable presets and templates. This can be particularly useful for musicians who are looking to expand their musical horizons and explore new creative possibilities.

Moreover, AI-generated music production tools can help musicians stay ahead of the curve by providing access to the latest trends and innovations in the music industry. By analyzing data from music streaming platforms and social media, these tools can provide insights into popular genres, artists, and songs. This can help musicians tailor their music compositions to meet the demands of their target audience and stay competitive in an ever-evolving industry. Additionally, AI-generated music production tools can help musicians discover new opportunities for collaboration and exposure by connecting them with industry professionals and influencers.

Overall, AI-generated music production tools and software offer a wealth of benefits for musicians looking to enhance their creative process and explore new musical possibilities. Whether you're a seasoned professional or an aspiring artist, AI technology can help you unlock your full creative potential and take your music to the next level. With the right tools and resources, you can create music that is both innovative and exciting, and make your mark in the ever-changing landscape of the music industry.

Examples of AI-Generated Music in the Industry

In recent years, artificial intelligence has made significant advancements in various industries, including the music industry. AI-generated music is becoming increasingly popular as a tool for artists, producers, and composers to create unique and innovative soundscapes. One example of AI-generated music in the industry is the work of Amper Music, a platform that uses machine learning algorithms to compose original music based on user inputs such as genre, mood, and tempo. This technology allows musicians to quickly generate high-quality music for their projects without the need for traditional music composition skills.

Another notable example of AI-generated music is the collaboration between IBM's Watson AI and Grammy-winning producer Alex Da Kid. Together, they created a song titled "Not Easy" featuring artists X Ambassadors, Elle King, and Wiz Khalifa. The song was created using AI algorithms to analyze popular music trends and create a track that would resonate with listeners. This groundbreaking project showcased the potential of AI in the music industry and opened up new possibilities for creative collaboration between humans and machines.

In addition to music composition, AI is also being used in the production and mixing of music. One company leading the way in this area is Landr, a platform that uses AI algorithms to master music tracks for artists. By analyzing thousands of songs and their corresponding mixes, Landr is able to automatically adjust levels, EQ, and compression to create a professional-quality master for any track. This technology has revolutionized the music production process, allowing artists to quickly and affordably master their music without the need for expensive studio equipment or a dedicated engineer.

AI-generated music is not just limited to traditional music production; it is also being used in other creative applications such as sound design for films, video games, and virtual reality experiences. Companies like AIVA and Jukedeck are using AI algorithms to create custom soundtracks for various media projects, saving time and money for producers and creators. This technology is transforming the way music is created and consumed, opening up new possibilities for artists and audiences alike.

Overall, AI-generated music is a powerful tool that is reshaping the music industry in exciting ways. From composition to production to sound design, AI is revolutionizing the creative process and enabling artists to push the boundaries of what is possible with music. As the technology continues to evolve, we can expect to see even more innovative and groundbreaking uses of AI in music production and beyond.

Chapter 4: AI's Impact on Graphic Design, Digital Art, and Fashion

AI-Generated Graphic Design Techniques

In recent years, AI-generated graphic design techniques have become increasingly popular among creative professionals. This technology allows designers to create high-quality visuals with greater speed and efficiency than ever before. By harnessing the power of artificial intelligence, designers can quickly generate stunning graphics that are tailored to their specific needs.

One of the key benefits of AI-generated graphic design is its ability to automate repetitive tasks. This means that designers can spend less time on mundane activities like resizing images or adjusting color schemes, and more time on creative tasks that require human ingenuity. By streamlining the design process, AI can help designers work more efficiently and produce better results in less time.

AI-generated graphic design techniques also open up new possibilities for experimentation and innovation. Designers can use AI algorithms to generate unique visual styles and effects that would be difficult or impossible to achieve using traditional methods. This can help designers push the boundaries of their creativity and create truly original and eye-catching graphics.

Another advantage of AI-generated graphic design is its ability to adapt to changing trends and preferences. By analyzing large datasets of design trends and user preferences, AI algorithms can help designers stay ahead of the curve and create graphics that resonate with their target audience.

This can be especially valuable in fast-paced industries like fashion and advertising, where staying on top of trends is essential.

Overall, AI-generated graphic design techniques have the potential to revolutionize the way we create visuals in the digital age. By combining the power of artificial intelligence with human creativity, designers can unlock new possibilities and create visuals that are more compelling, innovative, and impactful than ever before. Whether you're a seasoned professional or a newcomer to the world of graphic design, AI-generated techniques can help you take your work to the next level.

AI in Fashion Design and Trend Forecasting

In recent years, artificial intelligence has made significant strides in revolutionizing various industries, including the world of fashion design and trend forecasting. AI technology is now being utilized by fashion houses and designers to create innovative and trend-setting designs that cater to the ever-changing demands of consumers. By analyzing vast amounts of data from sources such as social media, runway shows, and consumer behavior, AI algorithms are able to predict upcoming fashion trends with a high degree of accuracy.

One of the key benefits of AI in fashion design is its ability to streamline the design process and reduce the time it takes to bring a product to market. By automating tasks such as pattern recognition, color matching, and fabric selection, AI-powered design tools can help designers bring their ideas to life more efficiently. This not only saves time and resources but also allows designers to focus on more creative aspects of the design process.

In addition to aiding in the actual design process, AI technology is also being used to forecast future fashion trends. By analyzing data from sources such as social media, online shopping behavior, and runway shows, AI algorithms can identify patterns and trends that may not be immediately apparent to human analysts. This allows fashion houses and designers to stay ahead of the curve and create collections that resonate with consumers.

Furthermore, AI is also being used to personalize the shopping experience for consumers. By analyzing data such as past purchases, browsing history, and social media interactions, AI algorithms can recommend products that are tailored to each individual's preferences and style. This level of personalization not only enhances the shopping experience but also helps brands to build stronger relationships with their customers.

Overall, the integration of AI technology in fashion design and trend forecasting has the potential to revolutionize the industry and drive innovation. By leveraging the power of AI algorithms, fashion houses and designers can create more relevant and impactful designs, predict future trends with greater accuracy, and personalize the shopping experience for consumers. As the technology continues to evolve, we can expect to see even more exciting developments in the world of AI-generated fashion content.

AI-Generated Digital Art and Illustration

Generative AI is revolutionizing the creative industries, allowing companies to produce high-quality video content, special effects, and entire marketing campaigns with the help of artificial intelligence. Major studios are now utilizing AI technology for tasks such as lip-syncing actors' performances in different languages and creating deepfake avatars for training and marketing purposes. This innovative approach to content creation is changing the way we think about storytelling and visual communication.

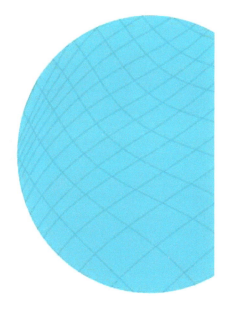

The Ultimate Guide to AI-Generated Video Content Creation

One of the most exciting applications of AI-generated content is in the realm of digital art and illustration. Artists and designers can now use AI algorithms to generate unique and visually stunning artwork in a fraction of the time it would take to create manually. These AI-generated pieces can be used for a variety of purposes, from advertising campaigns to social media content, and are helping to push the boundaries of what is possible in the world of visual arts.

AI-generated digital art is not only changing the way we create visuals, but also the way we consume them. By using machine learning algorithms to analyze trends and patterns in the art world, AI can help predict future trends in fashion design, product design, and even interior design. This information is invaluable for companies looking to stay ahead of the curve and create products that resonate with consumers on a deeper level.

In addition to creating stunning visuals, AI-generated digital art is also being used to enhance virtual reality experiences. By using AI algorithms to create realistic and immersive environments, developers can transport users to new worlds and create truly unforgettable experiences. This technology is revolutionizing the way we interact with digital content and is opening up new possibilities for storytelling and narrative creation.

Overall, AI-generated digital art and illustration are pushing the boundaries of what is possible in the creative industries. From generating high-quality video content to predicting future trends in fashion and product design, AI is revolutionizing the way we create and consume visual content. As this technology continues to evolve, we can expect to see even more groundbreaking applications in the world of art and design.

05

Chapter 5: AI-Generated Storytelling, Narrative Creation, and Product Design

AI-Generated Storytelling Techniques

The world of artificial intelligence is constantly evolving, and one area where it is making great strides is in storytelling. AI-generated storytelling techniques are revolutionizing the way content is created, particularly in creative industries. From generating high-quality video content to producing entire marketing campaigns, companies are utilizing AI to streamline the creative process and deliver innovative results.

One of the most exciting applications of AI-generated storytelling is in video content creation. Major studios are using AI to automate tasks like lip-syncing actors' performances in different languages, saving time and resources. Additionally, AI is being used to create deepfake avatars for training and marketing purposes, allowing for highly personalized and engaging content.

AI is also making waves in music composition and production, with algorithms able to generate original compositions in a fraction of the time it would take a human. This technology is revolutionizing the music industry, allowing for greater creativity and experimentation.

In the realm of virtual reality, AI-generated experiences are pushing the boundaries of what is possible. By harnessing the power of AI, developers can create immersive and interactive VR environments that captivate audiences and transport them to new worlds.

From graphic design to fashion trends, AI is transforming the way content is created and consumed. By leveraging AI-generated storytelling techniques, companies can stay ahead of the curve and deliver cutting-edge content that resonates with audiences. The possibilities are endless, and the future of AI-generated storytelling is bright.

AI in Product Design and Prototyping

AI in product design and prototyping is revolutionizing the way companies create and develop new products. With the help of AI technology, designers can now generate innovative and unique product designs in a fraction of the time it would take using traditional methods. AI algorithms can analyze vast amounts of data and user feedback to generate product designs that are not only aesthetically pleasing but also highly functional and user-friendly.

One of the key benefits of using AI in product design is its ability to quickly iterate and prototype new ideas. Designers can input their initial concepts into AI software, which can then generate multiple variations and options for them to choose from. This not only speeds up the design process but also allows for more creativity and experimentation, leading to better final products. AI can also analyze market trends and consumer preferences to help designers create products that are more likely to be successful in the market.

AI-generated product prototypes can also help companies save time and money in the development process. By quickly generating and testing different prototypes, designers can identify potential issues and make improvements before moving on to production. This reduces the risk of costly mistakes and ensures that the final product meets the needs and expectations of consumers. Additionally, AI can help companies optimize their production processes by identifying opportunities for automation and streamlining workflows.

Furthermore, AI in product design can also help companies stay ahead of the competition by enabling them to create products that are more innovative and cutting-edge. By leveraging AI technology, companies can tap into new design possibilities and push the boundaries of what is possible in product development. This can give companies a competitive edge in the market and help them stand out from the competition.

In conclusion, AI in product design and prototyping is a game-changer for companies looking to create innovative and successful products. By harnessing the power of AI technology, designers can generate unique and functional product designs, quickly iterate and prototype new ideas, save time and money in the development process, and stay ahead of the competition.

With AI as a powerful tool in their arsenal, companies can unlock new possibilities and drive creativity and innovation in their product development efforts.

Examples of AI-Generated Narratives and Products

In the realm of AI-generated narratives and products, there are countless examples of how artificial intelligence is revolutionizing the creative industries. One prominent use of generative AI is in the creation of high-quality video content. Major studios are utilizing AI to generate special effects, entire marketing campaigns, and even lip-sync actors' performances in different languages. This technology is also being used to create deepfake avatars for training and marketing purposes, showcasing the power and versatility of AI in video production.

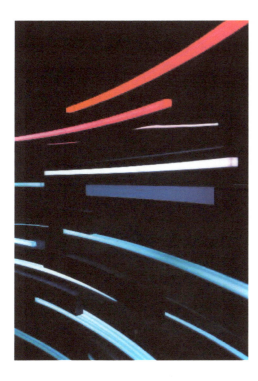

Another exciting application of AI-generated content is in the realm of music composition and production. AI algorithms are being used to compose original music, ranging from classical to pop genres. These compositions can be tailored to fit specific moods or themes, providing a valuable resource for musicians and producers looking for inspiration. Additionally, AI-generated virtual reality experiences are becoming increasingly popular, offering users immersive and interactive storytelling experiences that push the boundaries of traditional media.

In the world of graphic design and digital art, AI is making waves with its ability to generate stunning visuals and artwork. From creating intricate patterns and textures to designing logos and branding materials, AI is proving to be a valuable tool for designers looking to streamline their creative process. Similarly, AI-generated storytelling and narrative creation are being used to craft compelling narratives for various media, including books, films, and video games. By analyzing vast amounts of data, AI can generate engaging storylines and characters that resonate with audiences.

The Ultimate Guide to AI-Generated Video Content Creation

AI is also being used in the fashion industry for trend forecasting and design. By analyzing social media trends, runway shows, and consumer preferences, AI algorithms can predict upcoming fashion trends with remarkable accuracy. Additionally, AI-generated product design and prototyping are helping companies streamline their design process and bring innovative products to market faster. In the realm of interior design and architecture, AI is being used to generate realistic renderings and floor plans, allowing designers to visualize their projects in a virtual environment before construction begins.

Overall, AI-generated content is transforming the way creative industries operate, offering new possibilities for storytelling, design, and marketing. As AI technology continues to evolve, we can expect to see even more innovative applications in areas such as advertising, social media content creation, education, and training simulations. For people looking for a comprehensive guide to AI-generated video content creation, understanding the potential of AI in creative industries is essential for staying ahead of the curve and harnessing the power of artificial intelligence in your own projects.

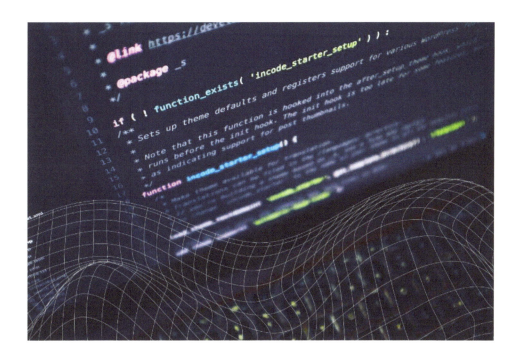

06

Chapter 6: The Future of AI in Interior Design, Architecture, and Advertising

AI-Generated Interior Design Concepts

AI-generated interior design concepts are revolutionizing the way designers and homeowners approach the creation of living spaces. With the help of advanced algorithms and machine learning, AI is now capable of generating innovative and sophisticated design ideas that can transform any room into a stylish and functional space. From color schemes to furniture placement, AI can provide endless possibilities for creating a personalized and aesthetically pleasing environment.

One of the key benefits of AI-generated interior design concepts is the ability to experiment with different styles and layouts without the need for expensive and time-consuming renovations. By simply inputting a few parameters such as room size, budget, and preferred aesthetic, AI can generate multiple design options that cater to the specific needs and preferences of the user. This allows for a more efficient and cost-effective design process, ultimately saving time and money in the long run.

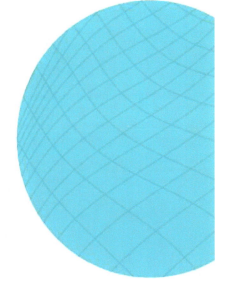

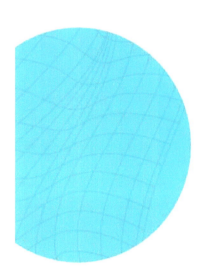

Moreover, AI-generated interior design concepts can also help designers and homeowners stay ahead of the latest trends in the industry. By analyzing data from various sources such as social media, online magazines, and design blogs, AI can identify emerging trends and recommend design elements that are in line with current styles and preferences. This ensures that the final design is not only visually appealing but also relevant and up-to-date.

Furthermore, AI-generated interior design concepts can also assist in creating cohesive and harmonious design schemes that reflect the personality and lifestyle of the occupants. By analyzing factors such as color psychology, spatial planning, and furniture arrangement, AI can ensure that every element in the room is carefully curated to create a balanced and harmonious environment. This attention to detail helps to enhance the overall aesthetic appeal of the space and create a sense of unity and coherence.

Overall, AI-generated interior design concepts are a valuable tool for designers and homeowners looking to create unique and personalized living spaces. By leveraging the power of AI, individuals can access a wealth of design ideas and inspiration that can help them transform their homes into beautiful and functional spaces. Whether you are looking to update your current decor or embark on a complete renovation, AI-generated interior design concepts offer endless possibilities for creating a space that is truly one-of-a-kind.

AI in Architecture and Building Design

AI has rapidly become an integral part of the architecture and building design industry, revolutionizing the way structures are conceived and constructed. With the help of generative AI, architects and designers can now generate innovative and cutting-edge designs that push the boundaries of traditional architecture. This technology allows for the creation of unique and personalized structures that cater to the specific needs and preferences of clients.

One of the key benefits of using AI in architecture and building design is the ability to optimize the design process and improve efficiency. AI algorithms can analyze vast amounts of data and generate design solutions that are both aesthetically pleasing and functional. By leveraging AI, architects can streamline the design process, reduce errors, and enhance collaboration between team members.

AI is also being used to create virtual reality experiences that allow architects and clients to visualize and interact with designs in a more immersive way. This technology enables stakeholders to explore different design options, make real-time changes, and gain a better understanding of the final product before construction begins. Virtual reality has the potential to revolutionize the way buildings are designed, allowing for greater creativity and innovation in the industry.

In addition to virtual reality, AI is also being used to generate interior design concepts that cater to the individual preferences of clients. By analyzing data on design trends, color schemes, and furniture styles, AI algorithms can create personalized interior designs that reflect the unique tastes and preferences of homeowners. This technology is particularly useful for architects and designers who want to offer customized solutions to their clients.

Overall, AI is transforming the architecture and building design industry, enabling architects and designers to create innovative and personalized structures that push the boundaries of traditional design. By leveraging AI technologies such as generative design and virtual reality, architects can optimize the design process, improve efficiency, and offer customized solutions to clients. As AI continues to evolve, we can expect to see even more groundbreaking advancements in the field of architecture and building design.

AI-Generated Advertising Content and Campaigns

AI-generated advertising content and campaigns have revolutionized the way companies promote their products and services. With the help of generative AI, marketers can now create high-quality video content, special effects, and entire marketing campaigns in a fraction of the time it would take using traditional methods. This technology is being adopted by major studios for tasks like lip-syncing actors' performances in different languages and creating deepfake avatars for training and marketing purposes.

One of the most exciting aspects of AI-generated advertising content is the ability to personalize campaigns for specific target audiences. By analyzing vast amounts of data, AI algorithms can tailor advertisements to individual preferences and behaviors, resulting in higher engagement and conversion rates. This level of personalization would be impossible to achieve manually, making AI an indispensable tool for modern marketers.

In addition to personalized content, AI-generated advertising campaigns can also be optimized for maximum impact. By continuously analyzing performance data in real-time, AI algorithms can make adjustments to campaigns on the fly, ensuring that messages are always relevant and timely. This level of agility gives companies a significant competitive advantage in the fast-paced world of digital marketing.

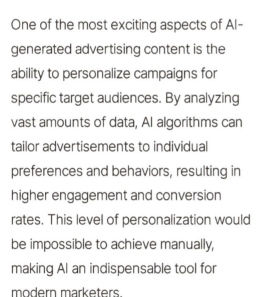

Furthermore, AI-generated advertising content is not limited to traditional formats like video and images. Generative AI can also be used to create interactive experiences, such as virtual reality simulations and augmented reality overlays.

These immersive experiences can capture the attention of consumers in a way that traditional advertising cannot, leading to higher levels of engagement and brand loyalty.

Overall, AI-generated advertising content and campaigns are transforming the way companies connect with their target audiences. By leveraging the power of generative AI, marketers can create personalized, optimized, and interactive experiences that drive results and stay ahead of the competition.

For people looking to stay at the forefront of marketing trends, understanding and embracing AI-generated advertising content is essential.

07

Chapter 7: AI's Role in Social Media Content Creation and Education

AI-Generated Social Media Content Strategies

AI-generated social media content strategies are becoming increasingly popular among businesses and individuals looking to streamline their social media marketing efforts. With the help of artificial intelligence, it is now possible to create high-quality, engaging content in a fraction of the time it would take to do so manually. This subchapter will explore some of the most effective strategies for using AI to generate social media content that will help you stand out in a crowded digital landscape.

One of the key benefits of using AI-generated social media content is the ability to personalize your messaging to target specific audience segments. By leveraging data analytics and machine learning algorithms, AI can help you identify the preferences and behaviors of your target audience, allowing you to tailor your content to resonate with them on a deeper level. This level of personalization can lead to higher engagement rates and ultimately, increased conversions.

Another advantage of AI-generated social media content is the ability to automate the content creation process. With the help of AI-powered tools, you can set up automated workflows that generate and schedule posts across multiple social media platforms, saving you time and effort. This not only allows you to maintain a consistent posting schedule but also frees up your team to focus on other important tasks.

In addition to streamlining the content creation process, AI can also help you optimize your social media content for maximum impact. By analyzing engagement metrics and user feedback, AI can provide insights into what types of content perform best with your audience. This data-driven approach can help you identify trends and patterns that can inform your content strategy moving forward, ensuring that you are always delivering the most relevant and engaging content to your followers.

Overall, AI-generated social media content strategies have the potential to revolutionize the way businesses and individuals approach social media marketing. By leveraging the power of artificial intelligence, you can create personalized, engaging content that resonates with your audience and drives results. Whether you are looking to increase brand awareness, drive traffic to your website, or boost sales, AI-generated social media content can help you achieve your goals more efficiently and effectively than ever before.

AI in Education and Training Simulations

AI technology has been making significant advancements in various industries, and one area where it is making a significant impact is in education and training simulations. AI-generated simulations are being used to create realistic and interactive learning experiences for students of all ages. These simulations can range from virtual reality experiences that allow students to explore historical events or scientific concepts, to interactive games that help students practice problem-solving skills.

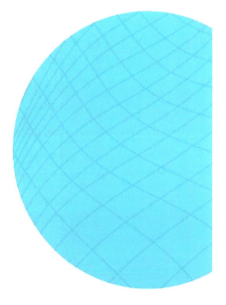

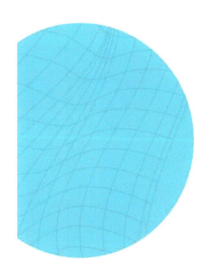

One of the key benefits of using AI in education and training simulations is the ability to personalize the learning experience for each student. AI algorithms can analyze a student's performance and tailor the simulation to their individual needs, helping them learn more effectively. This level of personalization is not possible with traditional teaching methods, making AI simulations a valuable tool for educators.

In addition to personalized learning experiences, AI-generated simulations can also help students develop important skills such as critical thinking, decision-making, and collaboration. By engaging with realistic scenarios in a simulated environment, students can practice these skills in a safe and controlled setting. This hands-on approach to learning can be especially beneficial for students who struggle with traditional classroom instruction.

Furthermore, AI technology is also being used to create simulations for training purposes in various industries. From flight simulators for pilots to medical simulations for healthcare professionals, AI-generated simulations are revolutionizing the way training programs are conducted. These simulations allow trainees to practice complex tasks in a realistic yet risk-free environment, enhancing their skills and confidence before entering the field.

Overall, AI in education and training simulations is transforming the way we learn and train. With the ability to provide personalized learning experiences, develop important skills, and offer realistic training scenarios, AI simulations are becoming an essential tool for educators and professionals alike. As this technology continues to advance, we can expect to see even more innovative applications in the future.

Examples of AI-Generated Educational Content

In recent years, generative AI has revolutionized the way educational content is created and delivered. From personalized learning experiences to interactive simulations, AI-generated educational content is changing the way students engage with information. In this subchapter, we will explore some examples of how AI is being used to create educational content that is both engaging and effective.

One example of AI-generated educational content is personalized learning platforms. These platforms use AI algorithms to analyze student data and create customized learning experiences based on individual strengths and weaknesses. By tailoring content to each student's specific needs, these platforms can improve learning outcomes and engagement levels.

Another example of AI-generated educational content is interactive simulations. AI-powered simulations can create realistic and immersive learning experiences that allow students to practice skills in a safe and controlled environment. From medical simulations to virtual science experiments, these simulations can help students gain practical knowledge and experience that would be difficult to replicate in a traditional classroom setting.

AI is also being used to create educational videos that are both informative and engaging. By analyzing data on student preferences and learning styles, AI algorithms can generate video content that is tailored to the specific needs of each student. These videos can cover a wide range of topics, from math and science to history and literature, and can be used to supplement traditional classroom instruction.

In addition to personalized learning platforms, interactive simulations, and educational videos, AI is also being used to create virtual reality experiences that bring educational concepts to life. By immersing students in realistic and interactive virtual environments, AI-powered VR experiences can enhance learning and retention by providing hands-on learning opportunities that engage multiple senses.

Overall, AI-generated educational content is revolutionizing the way we teach and learn. By leveraging the power of AI algorithms, educators can create personalized, interactive, and engaging learning experiences that improve student outcomes and prepare them for success in an increasingly digital world. Whether it's personalized learning platforms, interactive simulations, educational videos, or virtual reality experiences, AI is transforming education in ways we never thought possible.

08

Chapter 8: Conclusion and Looking Ahead

Ethical Considerations in AI-Generated Content Creation

In the rapidly evolving landscape of AI technology, ethical considerations are becoming increasingly important, especially in the realm of AI-generated content creation. As companies and individuals harness the power of generative AI for tasks such as video content creation, music composition, graphic design, and storytelling, it is crucial to address the ethical implications of using AI in these creative industries.

One of the primary ethical considerations in AI-generated content creation is the potential for bias in the algorithms used to generate the content. AI systems are trained on vast amounts of data, which can sometimes contain biases that are inadvertently incorporated into the generated content. For example, AI-generated music compositions may reflect the biases present in the training data, leading to potentially problematic outcomes.

It is essential for creators and users of AI-generated content to be aware of these biases and take steps to mitigate them.

Another ethical concern in AI-generated content creation is the issue of intellectual property rights. As AI systems become more sophisticated and capable of creating high-quality content, questions arise about who owns the rights to the content generated by these systems.

Is it the creator of the AI system, the user who inputs the parameters for the content, or the AI system itself? Clear guidelines and regulations are needed to address these issues and ensure that creators are fairly compensated for their work.

Privacy is also a significant ethical consideration in AI-generated content creation. As AI systems become more advanced, they have the potential to generate highly realistic deepfake videos and other forms of content that can be used to manipulate or deceive audiences. It is essential for creators and users of AI-generated content to be transparent about the origins of the content and ensure that it is used ethically and responsibly.

Overall, as AI technology continues to advance and become more integrated into creative industries, it is crucial for creators, users, and regulators to consider the ethical implications of AI-generated content creation. By addressing issues such as bias, intellectual property rights, and privacy, we can ensure that AI technology is used in a way that benefits society as a whole and upholds ethical standards in the creative process.

Future Trends in AI-Generated Video Content and Beyond

As we look towards the future of AI-generated video content, one trend that is expected to continue growing is the use of generative AI in creative industries. Companies are increasingly turning to AI to create high-quality video content, special effects, and even entire marketing campaigns. Major studios are utilizing this technology for tasks such as lip-syncing actors' performances in different languages and creating deepfake avatars for training and marketing purposes.

The Ultimate Guide to AI-Generated Video Content Creation

Another future trend in AI-generated video content is the use of AI for music composition and production. AI algorithms are becoming increasingly sophisticated in their ability to create original music, allowing musicians and producers to explore new sounds and styles. This trend is expected to revolutionize the music industry, with AI-generated music becoming more prevalent in mainstream media.

AI-generated virtual reality experiences are also on the rise, with companies using AI algorithms to create immersive and interactive VR content. This technology allows users to explore virtual worlds and environments in ways that were previously impossible, opening up new possibilities for entertainment, education, and training.

In addition to music and virtual reality, AI is also being used for graphic design and digital art. AI algorithms can generate stunning visuals and designs, helping artists and designers to push the boundaries of creativity. This trend is expected to continue growing as AI technology becomes more advanced and accessible to creators of all levels.

Overall, the future of AI-generated video content is bright and full of possibilities. With advancements in AI technology, we can expect to see more innovative uses of AI in industries such as fashion design, product prototyping, interior design, advertising, social media content creation, education, and training simulations. As AI continues to evolve, the potential for creativity and innovation in video content creation is endless.

Final Thoughts on the Ultimate Guide to AI-Generated Video Content Creation

In this final chapter of "The Ultimate Guide to AI-Generated Video Content Creation", we have covered a wide range of topics related to the exciting world of generative AI. From the basics of how AI-generated video content is created to the various applications across different industries, we have provided a comprehensive overview for people that want to delve into this cutting-edge technology.

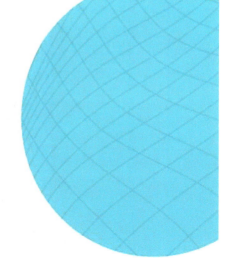

The Ultimate Guide to AI-Generated Video Content Creation

Generative AI is revolutionizing the creative industries by enabling companies to produce high-quality video content, special effects, and even entire marketing campaigns with unprecedented speed and efficiency. Major studios are now utilizing AI for tasks like lip-syncing actors' performances in multiple languages and creating deepfake avatars for various purposes. The possibilities are truly endless when it comes to what AI can achieve in the realm of video content creation.

Not only is AI being used for video content creation, but it is also making waves in other creative fields such as music composition, virtual reality experiences, graphic design, storytelling, fashion design, product prototyping, interior design, advertising, social media content creation, education, and training simulations. The potential for AI to transform these industries is immense, and we are only scratching the surface of what is possible with this groundbreaking technology.

As we wrap up this guide, it is important to remember that while AI-generated video content creation offers a plethora of benefits, it is crucial to approach this technology with caution and ethical considerations in mind. As AI continues to evolve and become more sophisticated, it is essential for users to be aware of the potential risks and implications of using AI in their creative endeavors.

Overall, the future of AI-generated video content creation is bright and full of exciting possibilities. By staying informed and keeping up with the latest developments in generative AI, individuals and companies can harness the power of this technology to create innovative and compelling video content that captivates audiences and pushes the boundaries of creativity. We hope that this guide has provided valuable insights and inspiration for those looking to explore the world of AI-generated video content creation.